Contents

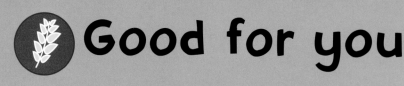

Good for you

Everyone needs to eat the right kind of food to stay healthy. The food we eat comes from plants and animals.

Many of the foods we eat are made from grains. Grains come from plants.

Grains and Cereals

Julia Adams

WAYLAND

Explore the world with **Popcorn** – your complete first non-fiction library.

Look out for more titles in the Popcorn range. All books have the same format of simple text and striking images. Text is carefully matched to the pictures to help readers to identify and understand key vocabulary.
www.waylandbooks.co.uk/popcorn

Printed in 2015

Dewey Number: 641.3'31-dc22
ISBN: 978 0 7502 9437 9
Library ebook ISBN: 978 0 7502 7615 3

10 9 8 7 6 5 4 3 2

FSC
www.fsc.org
MIX
Paper from
responsible sources
FSC® C104740

Editor: Julia Adams
Managing Editor: Victoria Brooker
Designer: Paul Cherrill
Picture Researcher: Julia Adams
Food and Nutrition Consultant: Ester Davies
Photo Models: Asha Francis; Lydia Washbourne

Wayland
An imprint of
Hachette Children's Group
Part of Hodder & Stoughton
Carmelite House
50 Victoria Embankment
London EC4Y 0DZ

First published in Great Britain in 2012 by Wayland
Copyright © Wayland 2012

An Hachette UK company.
www.hachette.co.uk
www.hachettechildrens.co.uk

Photographs:

Andy Crawford: 21, 22, 23; Getty: Dorling Kindersley 19; iStock: Grafissimo 4, nicolesy 5, dlerick 16; Shutterstock: juliengrondin 1/14, Pinkcandy 2/13, Suzanne Tucker OFC/6, Gorilla 7, Elena Elisseeva 8, Kodda 9, Terrance Emerson 10, Thomas M Perkins 11, OlegD 12, Denis and Yulia Pogostins 13, Yuri Arcurs 15, Sadeugra 17, Monkey Business Images 18, Kristiana007 20;

Grains are good for us because they give us energy. They also have vitamins and minerals that help us to stay healthy.

Bread is made from grains like wheat and rye.

What are cereals and grains?

Cereals are grass plants, such as wheat, oats and rice. They have a tall, thin stalk. At the top of the stalk, cereal plants grow seeds called grains.

Can you see where the grains are growing on these oat plants?

We cook grains in many different ways. Sometimes we boil them. A lot of grains from cereal plants are crushed, or ground, to make flour.

We use flour to bake bread and cakes.

Farming cereals

Cereal plants are grown on farms. The farmer plants cereals in huge fields. When the cereals are ripe, they are harvested.

When cereals start growing, they look just like grass. This is a field of wheat.

The grains are harvested by big machines called combine harvesters. Combine harvesters separate the grain from the rest of the plant.

This combine harvester is filling a tractor with wheat grains.

The little pockets that cereal grains grow in are called husks.

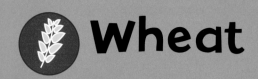

Wheat

The most popular cereal in the world is wheat. We use it to make many kinds of foods. It is often ground into flour in mills.

This is a mill. The tall towers are used to store flour.

We use wheat flour to make bread, pasta, pizza, pies, cakes and biscuits. It is used to make pancakes and to thicken sauces, too.

We make cookies using wheat flour.

Rye

Rye grains look very similar to wheat grains, but they are darker. Rye can be boiled and eaten instead of rice or in salads.

This is boiled rye. It has a slightly stronger taste than rice.

Rye is often ground into flour to make bread. Rye bread is very dense and darker than wheat bread.

wheat bread

rye bread

Can you see the difference between rye bread and wheat bread?

 # Rice

The fields that rice is grown in are called paddies. They are flooded with water.

The ripe grains are either picked by hand or by machine.

This farmer is planting rice seedlings in a paddy.

You have to boil rice to eat it. Many dishes from around the world use rice. Sometimes, rice is popped by heating it at a high temperature.

We eat popped rice as a breakfast cereal.

Can you think of a sweet dish that is made of rice?

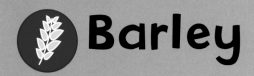 Barley

The grains of the barley plant are used to make both food and drink. We boil barley and add it to soups and stews. It can be eaten like rice, too.

Can you see the white barley grains in this soup?

Barley is also soaked and dried to make barley malt. This is added to drinks to make them sweet.

Squash is sometimes made with barley malt.

 # Oats

Oat grains are often steamed and then rolled into flakes. We eat oat flakes raw in muesli or cooked in porridge.

Porridge and fruit make a delicious and healthy breakfast.

Oat flakes are also used in baking.
Oatcakes, flapjacks, crumbles and
biscuits are made with oat flakes.

Oats are used to make the
crusty top of a crumble.

 Maize

We also call maize corn. It grows on cobs.

Each cob has **16** rows of maize kernels.

The dried kernels are used as grains.

Can you see the kernels on this cob?

Maize kernels are often ground into flour to make bread. They are also rolled and baked to make cornflakes.

Maize kernels can be heated and popped to make popcorn.

Fresh maize is also eaten as a vegetable. Then we call it sweetcorn.

Make your own muesli

Follow the steps of this recipe to make some delicious muesli for your breakfast.

1. Add the oats, the popped rice and the cornflakes to the bowl and stir with a spoon.

2. Add the pumpkin seeds and the sunflower seeds to the mix. You can add other seeds like sesame and flax, too.

3. Take a handful of dried apricots. Ask an adult to help you cut each of them in half. Add them to the mix.

4. Add the raisons to the bowl. If you like nuts, you can add a handful of mixed nuts as well.

5. To serve, add some fresh, cut fruit to your muesli and pour milk over it. You can also use yoghurt or fruit juice.

6. Enjoy your delicious breakfast!

Glossary

dense when something is tightly packed

harvest to pick a plant that is ripe

kernels the grains from a maize plant

mill a machine that grinds grains into flour

minerals substances in food that keep our bodies healthy. Calcium is a mineral that helps to build strong bones.

ripe when a plant is ready to eat

vitamins substances in food that help keep our bodies healthy and stop us from catching colds

Index